ENNEAGRAM

The Ultimate Guide to Understanding Yourself

(A Comprehensive Beginner's Guide to Learn the Realms of Enneagram)

Eugene Chagnon

Published By Bella Frost

Eugene Chagnon

All Rights Reserved

Enneagram: The Ultimate Guide to Understanding Yourself

(A Comprehensive Beginner's Guide to Learn the Realms of

Enneagram)

ISBN 978-1-77485-284-2

All rights reserved. No part of this guide may be reproduced in any form without permission in writing from the publisher except in the case of brief quotations embodied in critical articles or reviews.

Legal & Disclaimer

The information contained in this book is not designed to replace or take the place of any form of medicine or professional medical advice. The information in this book has been provided for educational and entertainment purposes only.

The information contained in this book has been compiled from sources deemed reliable, and it is accurate to the best of the Author's knowledge; however, the Author cannot guarantee its accuracy and validity and cannot be held liable for any errors or omissions. Changes are periodically made to this book. You must consult your doctor or get professional medical advice before using any of the suggested remedies, techniques, or information in this book.

Upon using the information contained in this book, you agree to hold harmless the Author from and against any damages, costs, and expenses, including any legal fees potentially resulting from the application of any of the information provided by this guide. This disclaimer applies to any damages or injury caused by the use and application, whether directly or indirectly, of any advice or information presented, whether for breach of contract, tort, negligence, personal injury, criminal intent, or under any other cause of action.

You agree to accept all risks of using the information presented inside this book. You need to consult a professional medical practitioner in order to ensure you are both able and healthy enough to participate in this program.

TABLE OF CONTENTS

INTRODUCTION 1

CHAPTER 1: WHAT IS ENNEAGRAM? 9

CHAPTER 2: KNOW THYSELF 21

CHAPTER 3: THE REASONS THE ENNEAGRAM IS IMPORTANT 41

CHAPTER 4: UNDERSTANDING THE BASIC PRINCIPLES UNDERLYING THE ENNEAGRAM 59

CHAPTER 5: INSTINCTUAL SUB TYPES 81

CHAPTER 6: APPLICATION OF YOUR GIFTS EVERYDAY 87

CHAPTER 7: THE STRUCTURE OF THE ENNEAGRAM DIAGRAM 102

CHAPTER 8: PHYSICAL APPEARANCE 123

CHAPTER 9: TYPE I THE REFORMER 130

CHAPTER 10: INSTINCTUAL VARIANTS **141**

CHAPTER 11: THE CENTER OF YOURSELF **150**

CHAPTER 12: THE ENNEAGRAM TYPE PERSONALITY 1 THE REFORMER **160**

CONCLUSION **182**

Introduction

The research into the inner workings of our mind has fascinated mankind for hundreds of years. It is, without doubt, the most complicated and intriguing organ in the universe. In contrast to the organs found in animals the capacity to think and think about our experiences and to anticipate the future and connect to a sense of spirituality is unlike any other creature that exists.

The way we think to identify personality differences and the factors that differentiate us from each other that are the basis of our individuality is an intriguing field of studying. However, a lot of this is explained using a unique analysis method known as The Enneagram. The accuracy of this system is awe-inspiring to thousands of people. We are amazed at how it can identify a certain personality type and the ease with which it can predict behaviours has led people to question whether there is some spiritual component that was incorporated into the program.

Everyday, people are searching for something more meaningful in their lives. In today's modern and dynamic world, the default is to look outside our own self to find that sense of meaning, which is unfortunate since the solution to the question of the person we are is not to have to do with the external world around us. Therefore, as many people are trying to find their meaning by praising others, in the thrilling adventures that life offers, or even at the bottom of a bottle or a drug some will be shocked to find that the true solution to who they are can be found within them.

Although these forms of external stimulation and self-fulfillment could offer some support and personal satisfaction However, the results they bring are usually fleeting. They don't nourish the core of our souls, the core of who we are. With this guide we will begin to look at ourselves through the eyes of wisdom instead of by physical connections. This book will provide you with the clarity you need to see patterns in the human being you are that you had never understood before.

The topic of this book is distinct in comparison to other self-help publications; the purpose isn't about "fixing" an unhappily person so that it can fit into the framework of contemporary society, but instead helps you discover who you are and how to fully embrace your person and find your true spot in the world. This is your right as a child.

If you'd like to be completely truthful with yourself, then the ability to recognize and interpret Enneagram individuals is the most crucial element that will allow you to connect with the true self which lies under the surface.

Unfortunately, a small percentage of people are aware of the inner being and do not appreciate its importance. In the modern age we are part of their surroundings that is focused on creating external connections and looking for personal fulfillment at same time. They do not have time to feed the inside of the person. In the past the idea of developing the spiritual part of us was an integral aspect of our lives However, as time passed and technology ushered in an instant gratification world The concept of a spiritual person was seen as something that was not compatible with the scientific method.

It's rare to find today's environments that support the idea of exploring one's spirituality as well as following the call of God. In fact it is more likely that people will be ridiculed for being ignorant and observing the old-fashioned traditions. However the ones who are brave enough to look into it, this path can help you integrate into the modern world we are living in. It is ironic that once we've discovered our unique Enneagram-like personality, a natural extension of that knowledge allows us to develop more positive relationships with others and to tackle the challenges with greater efficiency and live life at the top of the pyramid with other people with ease. It makes external connections more manageable and less stressful.

Here, we'd like to get you started on this journey. On the next pages, you'll learn:

A brief overview of Enneagram Personalities and how they got started

The Nine Basic Personality Types

How are they connected to one another

How do you find your social network

How can you apply this knowledge and incorporate it into your daily life

If you've had the moment of epiphany that moment when you suddenly know some aspect of you, something more profound than you've ever felt before, this realization arose from a deep thinking or simply a moment of reflection that gave an insight into what was hidden beneath the surface, it's probably an event that brought you to know you Enneagram personality. If you can remember how it is, get ready for more. The next pages will provide you with something much more potent than you ever thought of. Be prepared to meet in contact to the persona of your Enneagram Personality.

There are many books about this topic that are available, thank you to you for picking this one! The best effort was put into it to ensure it's packed with as much valuable information as is possible. Please have fun!

Chapter 1: What Is Enneagram?

Enneagram remains an unanswered question for many people. Although you are aware of the existence of various personality types, however, everything else remains a mystery. Yes, we see various personality tests and quizzes in magazines and online However, they're generally inaccurate. Keep in mind that such content is written solely to entertain and doesn't reflect the real personality of a person. Before you begin the process of discovering your character, it's crucial to be aware of the Enneagram and everything it encompasses.

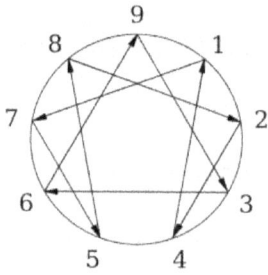

Enneagram overview

The word Enneagram originates from Greek word ennea (ennea) which means nine, in gramma (gramma) refers to something written or drawn. What exactly is it? The Enneagram is more than just the nine-pointed symbol, it is a powerful instrument for personal as well as collective transformation. It's an extremely specific system that categorizes individuals into nine personality types based on certain general diagnostic traits of their personality. The thing that makes the Enneagram system so intriguing is that individuals belonging to each of these types share numerous common traits, as well as distinct differences that distinguish each type apart from the others. Each personality type in the Enneagram spectrum is unique in its patterns of acting, feeling and thinking, which stems from an inner perspective or motive.

Image 1: symbol of the Enneagram (Photo source: Wikimedia Commons)

In the past of time, philosophers, scholars and other scientists have tried to define different types of people in order to explain their behaviours. Human nature is to seek to comprehend and explain how others behave, feel or think. The vast majority of personality classifications consider factors like religion, gender cultural, nationality, and religion. The Enneagram analysis goes beyond the notions about gender as well as other variables which allows for a better understanding of the human psyche and personality through the use of a universal language. What this kind of analysis could reveal is that while everyone is different and unique but we have many things that we share. The similarities with other people and our own individuality determine us and our view of the world that surrounds us.

It is easy to think of Enneagram as the consciousness map that underpins the entirety of an individual's life. It provides a thorough insight into the nine distinct personality types and explains the nine ways to live on the planet. Every personality type has its individual views on different aspects of their lives. You'll see throughout the publication, Enneagram is the key to understanding yourself and others. Although it could appear to be an intricate method for self-development it reveals the simplicity of our lives by helping you define your and other peoples behavior, thoughts and behavior. In addition, knowing how to understand Enneagram and the various personality types can give you an advantage in today's competitive business world of today.

The origins behind the Enneagram

The Enneagram isn't an invention of the past that aids us in understanding the other person's and our own personality. It's been around for a long time, which will only prove the importance of the model of personality. The truth is that the exact date of birth of the Enneagram is the issue of controversy because of different versions of its history and evolution due to the fact that it developed from an oral tradition. The first records of the personality Enneagram can be traced back to works of the Evagrius Ponticus an ascetic, Christian monk and ascetic, who lived in Alexandria at the time of the 4th century. Due to trade with various cultures, at that period Alexandria was a city with various spiritual and philosophical tradition.

Ponticus discovered eight dangerous thoughts called logismoi which include gluttony and abstinence in addition to fornication and chastity. greed and freedom, and possessions, joy and sadness as well as patience and anger as well as perseverance and acedia vainglory and the freedom from vanity pride and humility and jealousy as well as the freedom from jealousy. Monks also composed: "The first thought of all is self-love. following that, the eight." While the description of nine deadly thoughts seems contradictory, it's impossible to not notice the similarities between concepts and the Enneagram personality type. 1

In addition, several variants in the Enneagram symbol were discovered within the geometrical framework that was discovered by Pythagoreans who were intrigued by what the importance of numbers was and also their deep significance four thousand years before. The notion that numbers have more significance and the mysticism that goes with their significance was passed down through Plato and his student Plotinus and Neo-Platonists. The personality of the Enneagram is linked to the works from Philo of Alexandria who was a Hellenistic Jewish philosopher. In his writings the Enneagram tradition is described in the form of an image of the Tree of Life in the symbolism of ninefoldness , which is akin to Cabalistic principles. Furthermore, Philo frequently engaged in numerology that was inspired by Pythagoreans and was able to clarify the significance of the significance of the different numbers. Although the Enneagram transcends the boundaries of religion, it is important because it shows that the roots of this analysis of personality are all around us.

The origins of the symbol Enneagram are also traced back through its roots in the Muslim traditions or Sufi culture of Central Asia. It is believed that the Islamic tradition is known for its significant contributions to medicine and science. Sufis took wisdom from earlier traditions, including Hindu, Jewish, Platonic, Pythagorean, Christian, Buddhist,

Zoroastrian, and Taoist however, they made sure that the information didn't alter the concept of the Oneness of God and the idea of unity. The 14th century was the time when Sufism was founded by the Naqshbandi Order of Sufism known as the Brotherhood of the Bees and Symbolists kept and preserved the symbol of the Enneagram.

In actual fact, it's thought that the person who helped make the Enneagram popular George Ivanovich, a Russian philosopher, came across Sufis's tradition when he went to Sufis at the Sufi Sarmouni temple located in Afghanistan during the 20th century. He studied the process to understand different personality types and published his writings on the subject. The

Russian philosopher employed the Enneagram to explain the principles that govern the formation and development of the universe in every aspect of it. He also published his writings in the 1930s. While G.I. Gurdjieff is acknowledged as the one who put attention to the Enneagram it is important to point out that he didn't invent it , nor did he invent personality kinds. One of the people who came up with Enneagram theories of personality can be identified as Oscar Ichazo, a Bolivian-born philosopher and founder of the Arica School (human potential movement group).Ichazo assigned personality types to any of nine Enneagram positions and also described various kinds of personality types as well as their emotional concerns, and other characteristics during the 1960s.

In the 1970s, a trained psychiatrist from Chile, Claudio Naranjo, gave an extra boost to the recognition to the concept of an Enneagram persona as a part of the Western society. He thoroughly explored theories of personality and learned the work of Ichazo. His lessons at Berkley inspired others to pay greater consideration to self-development that was that was based on Enneagram personality kinds. Numerous other psychiatrists and philosophers have embraced this Enneagram tradition and have devoted more energy to the study of this vital aspect of human personality.

Chapter 2: Know Thyself

A cult shrines within Greece is the ancient'sanctuary of Delphi'.It was home to 150 quotes (maxims) in its walls. These maxims became called"the Delphic Maxims and they have created Greek thought and culture through the centuries.

The Greek writer, Pausanias, wrote the timeless phrase with just two words on front at the Temple of Apollo at Delphi. The most popular motto is 'Know Yourself' .It is the most popular and powerful of the 147 maxims , and the meaning was so significant it was that even one of the most famous philosophers of our time, Socrates too, expounded on the maxim.The idea could have been in widespread use for centuries, but just a few people on the earth can claim the fact that they have a complete understanding of the maxim in total.

The underlying question is the concept of personality in psychology and how we can apply it to our personal lives. Knowing your personal characteristics will help you identify the reasons you act in a certain way or what you do. Your behavior pattern isn't accidental and directly connects to who are. What we do and what we participate in don't happen by random chance, even though it appears to be. Therefore, it is important to attempt to understand yourself and take the difficult way of self-discovery.

In his study of the topic, he concluded "a life that isn't examined isn't worthy of living.' The great philosopher is telling that we should conduct an exhaustive analysis of our lives to uncover our character. The full list of the steps in your personal discovery will surely come as an unexpected surprise for you, and the reader may experience a revealing experience while reading this book.

Presently, there are more than seven billion people around the globe and each person is unique regardless of gender, age race, religion race, ethnicity or class. Each of us is unique as well. One of the primary ways we show our uniqueness is through our unique personalities.

"Personality" is a term used to describe the traits of psychology that differentiate one person from an individual. The traits aren't visible in terms of physical appearance except when they are manifested through the person's behavior. Personality can be described as the distinctive set of behavior that include cognitions, emotional patterns and cognitive processes which are derived out of environmental and biological patterns. The definition of personality reveals that it is a broad concept that includes the person's feelings, perceptions and behavior.

In the discipline of Psychology There isn't a "single recognized" term for personality, and there are many views regarding the topic. A certain group of psychologists study personality from the perspective of traits (characteristics that an individual has) and therefore believe that personality is the mixture of traits that we have as individuals. However other psychologists consider personality to be an identifiable pattern of behavior that defines an individual , or distinguishes them from other people.

It is therefore evident that our personality is based on our genetic characteristics and influences from the environment; we are a complex blend of nurture and nature, and decades of research in psychology prove this essential aspect of our personalities.

Certain indicators provide us with a glimpse into the core and character of our personality. Let's look at some of these points that we can look at our own inner-self :

Socializing with other people A person can be an introvert or extrovert. The introvert is more comfortable in solitude and is more likely to relax, whereas an extrovert likes the presence and the focus of other people. They each have distinct particular traits or traits. In addition, personalities come in various levels. There are two people who are introverts, but they are both more introverted. Similar to that, two people may be naturally optimistic but have certain characteristics greater than the other.

Learning style - Then is the fact that some people are visual learners who can absorb better with visual or graphic things, while some may be auditory learners that learn best when they are provided with materials for learning that include audio content. The child might not be able to do well in school, not because the child isn't talented, but rather because there aren't enough learning opportunities to support the way they learn.

Personal preferences - Some of us naturally cook or drive while another might not be a fan of these things, even if they are able to complete them. Personality traits vary so much among people that even twins can differ in many different ways. A person could be interested in an occupation in the field of humanitarian work , while his twin sister or brother might be interested in becoming a sports professional.

Individual differences in attitude - A person's mental disposition to behave in the way they do is a reflection of their personality. This is the principal reason for why individuals behave differently when faced with the same type of scenario. Psychology can help us comprehend the way that an individual's attitude can eventually affect their behavior. Someone who doesn't have any hint of arrogance within himself or herself will not behave in a hostile manner regardless of the challenge. However there are some people who have these tendencies, but they will not display it unless the circumstance requires it.

Human perception Most of the time you might not even realize that your personality can be seen in the way you view your surroundings. This is consistent with the popular phrase that "you do not perceive things in the same way however you perceive things in the way you see them." For instance, those who are honest can be more susceptible to being deceived because they believe in the opinions of others to be accurate. In essence, they view other people as they view themselves. Being honest and straight they have the same moral high standards from other people.

Unique habits - A person's routines, in many cases, give people an insight into their inner self and allows them to understand the type of person who hides behind the exterior skin. Everyone has habits that we love to engage in. They're integral to our identity. When it comes down to it, a person's routines will form the core of his or her personality. A person who is introverted will likely create a routine of staying inside as family and friends attend a party. Your actions therefore provide us with an idea of who you truly are.

Talents or "gifts of nature A person's natural talents and abilities will also give us insight into their character. Things that are natural to you, or the things that you can do easily are a sign of your personality or nature. One can master in just a few weeks the things that typically takes years to master. This indicates the ability and character of the person. In actual when someone continuously struggle to develop skills or proficiency in a certain area is an indication that might want to consider a different career.

Stress response - The way the way a person reacts to stressful situations can determine their personality. When confronted by danger, certain people will defend themselves, and others will decide to flee or move away from the situation. This is why you will see people who have a innate fear for animals, regardless of age or age in their lives. It can be difficult to change because it's a normal element of them. If you are stressed your fighting or flight response can give people an indication of the person you really are.

We have discussed ways that we can embark on the road of self-discovery we can now shift to discover what our personal personality and traits are formed. Below, I've provided a detailed explanation on two different ways that an person's personality develops. A person's personality develops by a mix of nurture and nature -

* The word "nature" is a representation of specific traits and behaviours that we have learned from our parents, or our predecessors. Certain traits are passed down genetically from parents to offsprings , albeit with minor modifications. Children may exhibit certain behavior patterns that clearly come from their grandparents or parents. They can be

extremely hard to "knock off" the person's lifestyle, even by their parents. Genetically-inherited behavior is able to be altered, but it is not completely removed.

"Nurture: It is the influences of our external environments. In our early years we are influenced by media, families and our beliefs about religion and the educational system, our peers, and on. We all are a product of our surroundings. Environmental influences are inevitable , no regardless of how hard we try to fight or resist it. This is the sole reason children who grew up in the ghetto or in a project is likely to behave differently than one who grew up in a wealthy environment even though they have the same genetic set.

Even though the subtle mix of our genes with our environment can determine what we become or are individuals, our personalities are able to change in time. For instance, you could naturally be shy and then, over time, learn to assert yourself in situations where you are required to. It is possible that you are unable to change your genetic makeup however your surroundings (whether intentional and/or not) can mentally and physically force you to behave in the way you want to. The way we behave isn't only dependent on environmental or genetic influences, but rather a mix of both.

It is crucial to note at this point that to understand our Enneagram personality takes a lot of effort from us and consequently, we should be active with the procedure. A biometric assessment of your physical characteristics may not require much personal input due to the participation of experts and technology. However, a psychometric test is completely different and is dependent in large part on the amount or quality and quantity of input. Psychometric tests are invalid if the answers you provide to the questions are not accurate. It's as if you were taking someone else's fingerprints instead of your own. The result do not provide an accurate representation of reality. Below are some methods that can be used in our thrilling and constant search for self -

Self-Introspection It's the art of taking your time to evaluate yourself. Being aware of yourself helps you improve your relationships and reduce conflict with other people. Reflection requires you to cast your eyes back to consider your unique behavior over time.

* Consensual feedback - Asking for feedback from those close to you, goes far in delving into the true you. Be open to accepting constructive criticism that can aid in growth. To receive constructive feedback, you have to be proactive and take the first step. Talk to people close to you to discuss certain aspects of your

personality , and ensure you receive honest feedback from them.

* Testing method - When you take tests for your personality that are legitimate and reliable, it could reveal a lot about you and help to understand the reasons behind your individuality. There are a variety of personality tests to suit a array of uses and are beneficial in all areas where crucial choices must be made throughout life such as marriage and careers, relationships education, business, and so and on. There are a variety of Enneagram assessments of personality are addressed in the next chapter; inquire locally about test of your personality in a locale near to you.

The careful examination of one's conduct by yourself or by a person who has been trained in the application of psychological methods or other related techniques. It is necessary to compare your behavior with the typical behaviour of different personality type and then decide which one best fits your personality. Although it's a challenge, may be, it can be rewarding if it is handled appropriately. The book there is a chapter dedicated to every one of the personality types within the Enneagram model, and allows you to dig deep into each one

Personality can be a complicated psychological construct , but taking a close review of the factors that constitute our personalities will help us comprehend and set us on the path of self-discovery. Both nurture and nature play crucial aspects of human character in various degrees, and typically the personality of a person is greater in one area but less. Also, you have a part to play in determining the persona you are.

The chapter we are discussing here we've looked at the following:

" * A powerful quotes in Greek philosophy that is a reference to our personality - "Know who you are"

* The essential role played by Self-discovery as a part of the way we live our lives

* The significance and composition of the human personality

* The debate between nurture and nature in understanding the human personality

In the next section we will explore the methodology of One of the world's most well-known personality inventories , the Enneagram. Being open-minded will assist you along this fascinating and insightful journey to self-discovery.

Chapter 3: The Reasons The Enneagram Is Important

This world can be a confusing world, and we design systems, or according to some we create systems to help us understand the world. The entire world is in problems with each other and, in reality that the reason is the lack of communication between every person. Being a frequent viewer of virtually every political drama that airs or in the past at least a little more about the politics and government functioning than I should. Madame Secretary, NCIS, (more of an procedural drama) The West Wing, Designated Survivor as well as many others are among my favorite shows I regularly check out for inspiration and information.

Sometimes, when watching these shows with wonderful characters, including I am aware of things.

People are having difficulty communicating. This is a common occurrence.

This is evident in government and politics between the leaders and the people who they govern, and their followers. The problem begins by misunderstandings, which are that is caused by the reality that our brains don't alike. Actually we're all completely different. Our identities are distinct, determined by the brain structure emotional structure hormones, body the genetics of our genes and much more.

We're all unique and all cut and constructed from different materials. But the truth is that we're all cut from the same cloth. It's where I, for myself am able to find optimism. We can all discover hope. We're all human beings and all of us have fairly standard desires and needs. We're clearly distinct from each other due to of our unique personal identities but at the root of it all, we're any different. Our individuality isn't a problem, but at the final analysis, we're all the same. Many of us are in similar categorical categories which is the point where the Enneagram is a factor. We're all cut from various kinds of fabric, but we're all made of the same stuff.

We're all made of cloth, cut in a different way.

This is where the Enneagram is able to transform your life and turn your life upside down.

We're all different and different from everyone else but we're all humans. We all have weaknesses, strengths desire, emotions, thoughts and goals. Are you prepared? Get ready to know much more about you than you had before. Perhaps you can take a look at some different ways of handling other people. A final thing to note before we dive into the subject. I'd like to talk about how the Enneagram is distinct from other system, and how it demonstrates no bias, gets right to the core of problems, and offers the chance to connect the other personality indexes. Myers-Briggs is a vital system that has played a huge impact on my life as I mentioned in the previous section.

Through the rest of this book , I'll use a variety of examples of characters, including some that I've developed and written about in addition to characters from television shows, books and films. The process of creating characters is a lengthy process. It all starts by creating a picture within your head, and then contemplating what they appear like, what they look like, who they are as well as what they represent the is their story and how they react to the events around them and those surrounding them. I have come up with a variety of diverse characters in the last several years, and from the perspective from Myers- Briggs. It helps explain the behavior. It is also true that the way you behave can define and convey motivation. In many cases, we are able to draw conclusions from what we hear from the mouths people around us as well as the way they react to certain situations and words and the decisions they make in the course of their lives, and much more, to gauge the motivation.

Behavior, as revealed by MBTI is explained by the Enneagram that goes one step further. However, there is a second "personality index" which is a part of this discussion too. Harry Potter, a book and film series that is among my personal favorites is one of my top choices not only because of the amazing characters and amazing filmmaking skills in addition to the plot of the writer, but also because of the Hogwarts houses, which is thought to be a personality type method of its own.

Hogwarts homes are an popular system utilized by millions of people across the globe. A lot of people had read books or seen the films, and then began to decide which house they belonged to and then discover and identify their identity using the magic Sorting Hat.

But, the reason why Enneagram differs from the Hogwarts Houses system Hogwarts Houses is due to the fact that Enneagram does not have good as well as bad ones like the house system of Hogwarts houses. Within the Harry Potter universe, the house of silver and green is known as the Slytherin house, is frequently considered to be slimy and sluggish people. In essence, they're compared to snakes. Hufflepuff, in contrast is a badger, fragile, meek, and loving. The Ravenclaw are decent and noble, however, they're not as great as the final house. Gryffindor is the home of most of main character, and often thought of as the favorite of the public and regarded as the most desirable. This isn't necessarily an issue, since this is because the Harry Potter series, after all, is a collection of tales of fiction created to entertain the audience.

My problem regarding my experience with Harry Potter Houses is that individuals decide what category they belong to, and then leave it to them. However there's a need for a certain.

If you're looking to become the top, and if you're looking to be in the House of the main characters You must have the status of a Gryffindor. If you're Slytherin, then you'll most likely be perceived by peers among Harry Potter fans as a snake-like individual, with evil motives and unsavory methods of making yourself more prominent within the world. We can think of this from the perspective that of Enneagram for a minute. Perhaps your favorite character on television is one of the Four. You've seen them, You love them and admire them and appreciate their traits and character. You'd like to be like fans would like to call it "be the same as them".

It could be an actual person, perhaps your favorite writer, actor or creator. You've seen them and their supposed Enneagram number , and you believe that, to be included as a member of their group you have to be in the same category as they are. This isn't actually the scenario. Some years ago, I crafted one of my top artworks ever. It was quite unusual given how poor as an artist am I in any area of art aside from photography or writing. I printed several images depicting fictional female characters (and Alex Morgan, a professional soccer player because she has incredible legs I admire) as well as a few images of characters I was awed by, and put them all together to create an affixed poster that featured the phrase, "I will not live for the rest of my life with regret" which is by Penny Chenery in the movie Secretariat.

After I uploaded a picture of the project on Instagram and this was the caption"Another day, another project. These are only a few of my idols women who have displayed qualities and passions that I'd like to participate in. While I'm not aiming to be one of them, it would be incredible to be included among their group of followers. In the Enneagram there's no favouritism.

There isn't a perfect person like there is no one who is perfect. Like my Instagram post stated that we don't need to be like other people We should take the traits and values we like about them the most and apply these to our lives in a manner that is best suited to our lifestyle and outlook on the world. The women on the board come from many different walks of life and they all have different Enneagram number.

If you go to the official website for the Enneagram Institute, you'll find many interesting information. The site is amazing and has many resources that are essential to your development however, one of my top picks is their list of different levels of growth of the various types. Each of nine kinds provide Nine levels of growth for each level, with Level Nine being the lowest and weakest, with One being the highest. Numerous famous individuals of every type who are popular and respected are have the highest levels of development in their particular category of motivation and personality. Superheroes and heroes generally and world leaders, historic famous individuals are all who are at the top. The beauty is that they come of all kinds and sizes.

The beauty and significance of Enneagrams is that it is no capacity to choose the most popular.

Although the fact that I am a particular number, may get along better than others however, I am no better than anyone else. Every type has its distinct strengths and weaknesses. There isn't a perfect kind. There's no perfect type. It's all about the person and what they can achieve in their personal development and progress. It's your responsibility rather than your number to assess your capacity for growth, success and integration into this life. Your potential to be successful and be successful, well-known, and an effective leader, isn't determined by your Enneagram numerology.

There is no advantages or disadvantages in the society because of your Enneagram. at the very least, not by nature. It is the Enneagram is, again it's about your tendencies or your motivation and your thinking and your thoughts and not about your potential and capabilities or something similar. Everyone's on the same field. However, we all reach our maximum level of growth by relying on our own numbers and in a different way. It is important to be aware that our personality isn't an reason to be able to justify. The most important thing to remember to consider when examining the different traits and personalities is to recognize that everyone is at a different point of development.

As we were having a discussion at dinner with friends the subject of Enneagram was brought up. Since we all came from different paths in life as women and men and that our differences were glaring and arousing, it was a fascinating conversation, with plenty of unresolved questions at the end which was when we were forced to split up because of the current. A lot of comments were offered by those who were in favor of the theory. They discussed who they believed to be or mistyped and there was plenty of general discussion about what we were all about and the people we were and the way we behaved in various situations.

As expected there were some doubters.

One of the younger men who were in the room made a statement about how he does not dislike people who make remarks regarding how, "Oh, I do this because I'm a _____." Then I informed me that I totally believe in. The process of determining your personal numbers, your position in the spectrum of personality behavior, motivation, and personality is about understanding the underlying causes and then moving in a positive direction with the knowledge you have gained. It's as if you're looking over an outline of a map.

You don't say "YOU are here" and think "Great You're in my place." Instead, you tell yourself, "I'm here and I'm going to go there, this is how I can make this happen."

However it's impossible to get the direction you'd like to go until you know your current position. The end goal, or the destination that you're working towards is precisely where the levels are. Levels of the Enneagram are an eye opener, as well as an inspiration to me as well as others. In looking at the type for my personal number, as well as examining the who are famous in my particular category of Enneagram My eyes were opened up to what I could become. I realized how I would like to think about things as well as which strengths I have to be used for, what I'll need to do to achieve them, and what I can improve my strengths, talents capabilities, and Godgifted talents. That's the reason why the Enneagram is important. Then, let's look at the various types...

Chapter 4: Understanding The Basic Principles Underlying The Enneagram

There's a good chance you've been a victim of the opinions of numerous experts about the Enneagram. As you've gathered, it's a symbol that is shrouded in mystery and significance, and the significance of its various components are not always comprehended. This is what makes it hard for some people to believe in the concept; and the absence of an explicit explanation of the whole procedure frequently leaves people suspicious and sceptical, believing they might be entering the realm of occultism.

For many people, the occult is what they are thinking of when they look at an Enneagram symbol. Our minds immediately think of it because it is so similar to the pentagram. It is in direct relation to the modern occult. Many people are hesitant from worry that they might be involved in something extremely mysterious and obscure. But, by looking at the image without beliefs and clearing your mind of the ideas people are prone to immediately connect with it, we can begin to recognize some commonalities we can see in more common beliefs in our society.

It's an inherent part of us to want to learn more about the roots of everything we are involved in. Even though the explanation for the symbol can appear ambiguous and unclear but we've managed to discover enough information to reveal the meaning behind it. Enneagram symbol. It could take a bit of searching to discover the meaning within the various elements however it's worth the effort to investigate.

It is important to note that the Enneagram that we employ in the present has evolved from its initial purpose. One of the best methods to determine its meaning is beginning with the human brain. It's a normal tendency for the human brain to see images and then divide them into various categories. This isn't anything fancy, it's the way our brains are created to do. As Gurdjieff was believed to be the founder for the current Enneagram and many people automatically identify with the current Enneagram as a symbol of his. The teachings of Gurdjieff were heavily influenced by the metaphysical as a way of organizing the natural laws and applying them to describe how the universe operates.

Three basic principles were part of Gurdjieff's metaphysical theories, all of them based on an Enneagram symbol. It is the Law of Seven, Unity and The Law of Three.

It is the Law of Seven: this law was focused on the continuous motions that we all experience around us. It's distinct from Newtonian Physics we've learned from the latest science. In contrast to what we've taught that an object that moves remains in motion and never stops moving, the

Law of Seven sees the world as a series of resonant vibrations. In accordance with this law, every object in motion must undergo seven different phases before coming to a complete stop. This means that energy that is expended is not evenly and is instead being lost at specific locations before it is able to receive an additional injection of energy in order to continue on its course.

His theory was based upon the musical octave of seven notes and the notion that in nature once things are moving the motion can't continue for ever. However, whatever you call it, the speed has to be altered or diverge at certain intervals. While you traverse the musical scale, for instance when the vibrations of energy increase as they decrease or increase, the steady rate will naturally change at specific places. When it comes to music, the points are classified as the mi/fa points and the si/do point. Also, in an octave do re mi-fa then ti do. The intervals during which vibrations change will occur between the mi and the Fa at a particular place, and between the si and do at a different place.

Of course, there's plenty more to the idea that is the Law of Seven that we will not discuss here.

According to Gurdjieff energy that is expended in vibrations doesn't dissipate uniformly and is instead lost at specific points, that it may be redirected to continue along its route.

Unity Infinity at the Enneagram symbol the eyes automatically identify that circle as the first. It is the universal symbol for unity and the infinity. It also symbolizes the unity and eternal nature of the Supreme Being. For Gurdieff, the circular shape was a symbol of two different ways of thinking. First, all of the universe has a home and everything is part of the same universe without exception. The symbol was employed to stimulate an expansive and more open consciousness of the whole. It is done without judgment or labelling anything as good or evil. Anyone who is able to do this will be able to be able to see the world as it is as it is as well as not being affected by preconceived notions and personal opinions.

It is the Law of Three or the Triangle The Law of Three or the Triangle symbolizes the unification of three basic things. In the first place the supreme Being in the Universe (God) determines its character and its structure. Second, its organizing principle and, finally, the power that God can use to bring everything together. These three elements are essential to understand Gurdjieff's teachings about The Law of Three.

It is evident that the teachings of Gurdjieff were extremely intricate and thorough, however understanding the fundamentals is the first step to be able to comprehend the purpose that the symbols serve. Human beings are always in a state of confusion. On one hand, we're constantly seeking our individuality, but on the contrary, we feel an inborn need to be part of something greater than us. As the western world shifted more about the person to the point that almost everything was disconnected and the east fought to connect and community almost completely obliterating the individual.

If you look at the world through a lens that is more given to connections The price you pay is the loss of dignity for a human being that is sacrificed for the good of the entire. However in situations where too much importance is placed on an individual, the result is the denial of the rights of other people. So, being able to find a balance between the two is vital and having the spiritual being in charge of it is essential.

As a supreme being that is both one and diverse, unity and diversity can play an equal role in our lives. we can learn to live our lives for each other and for the world around us.

Although the origins of this symbol might appear elusive and unclear but our current understanding of the symbol could provide us with a more clear significance. The more we know about it and its meaning, the better we will be able to remove the doubts about its mysterious and dark roots. Nowadays, the symbol is often used as a symbol of many different people.

The symbol we use in the present isn't exactly identical to the symbol that he had in mind (it is refined through time to make it more appropriate to the modern society.) It can be used in a variety of ways when you take it apart. There are a variety of options for how to make use of the symbol. With all the different personalities , it can be hard to determine the place you're at in the spectrum of personality. When you've finished this book, you'll be able to get a good insights into the knowledge of the Enneagram and will be able to determine precisely where you are into the larger world of things.

Today's Enneagram

As we've previously mentioned that the layout of an Enneagram is essentially the form of a circle, with lines and numbers inside it. Each of these circles, numbers and lines can be studied and examined from different angles. In the most basic

Enneagram symbols, one will initially observe a circle that has numbers from one to nine around the perimeter in like the way numbers are arranged around the clock.

It's easy to see that the notion of a circle that has drawn lines that are numbered doesn't convey much. It isn't until you learn what each marking actually mean. In the fundamental Enneagram symbol the circle represents an omen of unity. The nine types of personality are equally spaced from one another, showing that they are all equally each other. Each personality has more influence or influence over one another. We all start on an identical footing.

If you pay attention you'll see an inner triangle created by joining the points that are located at the numbers 3 six, nine, and three. This triangle symbolizes a powerful and dynamic interaction between three forces.

The Circle: You'll find nine distinct points scattered around the circle's circumference. We know that the circle represents of unity. The 9 points in the circle are equally from each other. This means that each person is the same, yet still linked to one another.

The Triangle The Triangle: If you examine carefully, you will notice an inner triangle connecting the three points of three, six and nine. It is a dynamic interaction between three strong forces. If you take two opposites for instance the force that connects two of them would be a type of middle ground or a mix of all of the opposites of polarity. Three Enneagram Clusters have been joined through the triangle.

Hexad In the event that you examine the image further you'd also see an odd figure connecting all the other six points. This symbol symbolizes the constant change we all have to go through. As you'll discover in the next section every person has their own distinct personality, however it is not at all times in control of the time. We all switch between personalities and each is symbolized by the Hexad that connects them all.

The Numbers The nine numbers that are around the circumference represent nine personality kinds. Each type has the motivational seeds of its own which triggers certain actions. Although we all share several different personality types, we all have a primary or more powerful Enneagram type that is the one that determines our own personal beliefs about life as well as the actions we choose to take and the way we react to the environment that surrounds us.

The Arrows The Arrows: What you might not be able to see in many Enneagram symbols is the Arrows. But, if you look at ones with arrow tips on the top of the lines, you'll see that they are based on an exact pattern that illustrates the way people change their personalities in various situations. When you're stressed and confident, or are achieving the personal growth you desire and development, your behavior naturally and instinctively change from one persona to another within your Group. Then, we will travel along those connecting pathways following the direction of the Arrows.

The arrows that move backwards represent your stress-related personality, which is the way you automatically go about getting away from your usual behaviour and preventing emotional harm. If some people are under severe anxiety, they can shift to this point of stress and stay there for days and weeks, even months and even years, before they are confident enough to return to their normal personality.

However the arrows that point forwards are towards a more secured location that permits you to engage in more safe behaviors. When you're at your security level generally, you're in an environment that who you count on. If you're in good health it is possible to decide to move towards an Integration Point. This is where you mix with qualities that create an ideal balance between structure and confidence. If you're trying to grow in your career, it's essential to accept this Security Points and follow those good habits in your daily life.

At this point, you've likely started to realize that you belong to one particular personality type. In fact, you've likely identified a number of. If you're looking to determine what your Personality Type have, there are many websites which can assist you. A few of them are completely free , but the ones that are that are worth your time will cost you a amount of money to test. But the knowledge that you gain from this knowledge could be beneficial to you and help enhance your life in many different ways. We'll list these towards the end in the text.

It's easy to understand the reason why people are fascinated by The Enneagram and what it could be to their lives. This tool allows you the opportunity to look at your life and discover what it is. It gives you the ideal perspective for looking at your life from a different angle and identifying patterns that have influenced your choices since you were born.

With this new knowledge of yourself, you'll be more confident in venturing into other areas that are outside your comfortable zone. If you are able to do that the right thing, your purpose in life will be more clear and your path through life, your future will unfold in front of you. The process of discovering your Enneagram personality is as much an intellectual journey in the same way as it's a mental one. However, when you approach the journey with an open mind it's possible for you to gain more understanding of the human mind and find your own destiny. But, it's going to need you to look into the depths of what's in your soul to discover your true nature.

The Iceberg

Humans are highly sophisticated creatures and are comprised of various elements. Although we all share the same elements however there is a unique blend of these components that makes us unique. Your persona is composed of a delicate mix of a variety of elements that reflect not only your emotions and experiences, but also manifests in the way you present your self and interact with people who surround you. Each element has a distinct purpose in building your personality in you.

It is often described as an Iceberg. Although the iceberg is huge in its size, the elements you observe above the water are the things that you are conscious of. This is the part of us that we let others observe. But, the majority of who we are is below the surface, the part of us that we don't know about or the part we are trying to hide from people who are in our lives.

These hidden aspects are what motivate us to engage in certain actions. To put it simply the hidden aspects of our personalities can be described as aspects that we experience, while those that are visible to us can be thought of as the factors that influence us and which we are conscious of how we react to. All of these influences influence our behavior and provide the motivation to perform what we do.

To allow to allow the Enneagram to be the most efficient and beneficial to us, it is essential to consider what lies between as well as below. The combination of both gives us the understanding and wisdom to make the necessary changes that we might feel we require to make to improve.

Chapter 5: Instinctual Sub Types

Synopsis

The person's dominant nature can be altered or dependent on the people around them. This is manifested as an individual "wing".

It is believed that there exists a design which affects the enneagram type greatly apart from the wings. It is the sub-type that has the most instinctual.

Offshoots

* If you're a type 2, you might have a wing that is type 1 or type 3.

* This could be described as an 2 with wing 1 or the 2 with wing 3.

* If you're Type 9, then you could have a type 1 or type 8.

* This could be described as an 9 with wing 1, or 9. wings 8.

Someone who is heavily at the mercy of one side has just one of their wings. Someone who is at the mercy of both sides (or not whatsoever) is thought to be an individual with healthy wings or "no wings' (meaning that they are an individual of their dominant type , without the influence of their neighbour).

No matter how powerful the wing of a person will be, it won't change the essence that is the predominant personality.

In the sense that two people could have the following traits:

* 2 with wings 3, (Helper With Achiever Wing)

* 3 with wing 2. (Achiever and Helper Wing)

Both are very different from each other even though they have the same dominant style and wings.

One way to describe the situation is to say that you will always find chocolate-flavored Ice cream, but it's totally different from an Ice cream with chocolate flavor - so the CORE type never changes , and neither perform their primary function.

The subtypes are usually the manifestations of an individual's innate nature when they interact in the real world.

The energy of the instincts is manifested in such a way that every person who is the dominant type of personality can manifest their energy and instincts in different ways.

The 3 basic instincts are:

Self preservation is a variant.

The sexual or one-to-one variation

The social variation

Self-preservation individuals tend to be more focused on their personal security as well as their health natural resources such as their nest eggs, health, and tend to be more reserved than the sexual or social variety.

Sexually inclined people tend to concentrate heavily on the chemistry, or the bond between an person and the other. They're not motivated by sexual drives, however, they are more interested in ways to express their feelings by expressing intimacy or a deep emotional bonds. In contrast to the social sub-type they are more likely to have close friends or an close relationship.

Social people, on the other hand, aren't so focused on the primary intimacy. They are able to function in groups and tend to lean toward many connections with friends instead of intimacy or intensity. It is believed that, when the child is born, they should feel secure, safe and well-fed. The inability to meet this requirement throughout the course of childhood results in an individual developing a self-preservation mode that is primarily focused on their individual survival.

If the child's physical and security requirements are met, but the emotional connection is not there one could be able to develop into sexually inclined in their search for intimacy with other people, which usually isn't the case as a child growing up with either or both of the parents.

If both requirements are satisfied, they will become healthy social creatures. There are some exceptions to this general rule of education, but it's generally a common pattern across subtypes.

Chapter 6: Application Of Your Gifts Everyday

While you are working on ways to improve your empathy abilities and abilities, you will need to learn more about how to apply these skills in your daily life. This chapter will explain how you can start taking your growth to the next level , and start enjoying a greater sense of happiness and empowerment through your empathic abilities. Integration at this level helping you to begin to conquer some of the more difficult issues you've had to deal with throughout your life so you can enjoy yourself again.

Finding Out Where Your Day Can Be Improved

The first thing you're likely to be required to do to integrate your empathic abilities in your everyday life is to start looking for areas in your day that could be enhanced. As empaths, you might have become so used to spending every day stressed out as well as overwhelmed. You might not even know of when and where these feelings begin to seep into your daily life. Being aware of the source of these energy surges from, what they are, when and how they feel as they start aid in getting clear on the things you'd like to enhance with the daily routine of your integration.

An empathic journal can be an excellent way to identify areas of your life in which you are influenced by your strengths to determine the areas you'd like to put your efforts when it comes to taking them into your life. Keep an e-journal or even in your phone. You note the time of day when your energy came up, what was going on and what you were thinking and how you felt. After a few weeks you'll start to observe patterns in your energy, indicating where you are absorbing unwelcome energy, and the ways you may be making yourself open to these specific kinds of energy.

You are granting yourself permission to begin one step at a time

The next step to incorporate your empathic talents into your everyday life is to give yourself the permission to take it on at your pace. A major errors empaths commit is to alter their lives in a single moment. This although admirable, can be stressful and stressful. As you use your abilities to help you instead of allowing others to utilize it to exploit you, there will to be some challenges that you must face. You will have learn to deal with the energies of others as they become discontent with their inability to take advantage of you, which is a process that takes time to get used to. At first, you could be tempted to give in, despite having the most effective techniques in place. This may cause anger and frustration in you, and the need to take a step back from the negative energy of another. The ability to take things slowly and make a few mistakes throughout the process ensures that you don't make your expectations too high and take more than you're able to chew.

The best way to grant yourself permission to do so and actually believe it, is to declare that you're accepting your right to move through things slow and in your individual pace. Create an affirmation that you'll apply whenever you are in a situation in which you have to grant yourself the permission to slow down and take the situation at your own pace. If, for instance, you find yourself in a position in which you find yourself regularly being a victim of others who are trying to take advantage of you, grant yourself the right to take it at your own pace , and try to alter the situation as much as you can. If you are having difficulty making changes Take the stress off by telling yourself that there's no requirement to make it right the first time. As you become more adept at creating shields and establishing limits and boundaries, the easier it will be to do it with more confidence and determination when you need to do it again. There's no harm in taking it slow and going at your own pace and don't be scared to repeat your mantra whenever you feel like you're not being truthful. Be patient with yourself.

Steps to Integrate your Empathic Talents Daily

It is now time to find out what it's like to begin incorporating your empathic talents in your everyday life! The way this is implemented each day will differ, based on the situation you're in and what you expect from you in these scenarios. Therefore instead of providing you with an agenda or a schedule of how to integrate your empathic abilities into each day life I will offer some ideas that you can follow to begin making it a part of your unique experience. After that, you can begin trusting these tips whenever you require to navigate different situations and gain more confidence and peace in your daily life!

Step 1. Review your Energy of the Day

First thing that you could do each day, aside from establishing your shield and settling yourself, is to examine the energy of the day. Many empaths have reported being capable of feeling the vibe of a day, based on the energy the collective has released. If you spend some time reading about this energy every morning could aid in gaining a better understanding of the challenges you could have to experience in your day-to-day tasks.

You can determine the energy of a particular day in your morning routine by asking your inner voice what energy patterns are present in that particular day and how they could affect your life. It is important to consider whatever information you receive intuitively even if it may not be logical to you at the moment. There may not be any terms that you could use to express what the energy of the moment is however, you may feel an impression of your own which gives you some idea about what you can anticipate. It's enough to provide you with an idea of what energy to watch out for and the ways you could be able prepare yourself to deal with them by knowing that they will come up.

Step 2. Read the energy of People

Another thing you should think about doing daily is to study the energy of people you interact with. The act of slowing down at the beginning of each meeting and taking a moment to look at the energy of people who are around you will provide you with the chance to gain an understanding of how they could be feeling at the time. This will aid you in getting an understanding of what your interactions might be but also where the energy might be coming from if you begin to notice unusual feelings in your body. For instance, if are aware that your spouse was extremely happy this morning and you've experienced an undisclosed sensation of joy throughout the day This could be due to the energy you picked up from your spouse.

It is also possible to make use of this occasion to analyze the attitude of the people you meet in order to decide if they're a good fit to connect with and communicate with. If you're looking to establish new friendships or networks with new acquaintances such as yourself you can utilize your senses to determine whether it's going to be a pleasant experience. This is a fantastic method of gaining insight the energy of energy parasites, such as narcissists, earlier so that you be wary of forming friendships with them at the beginning.

Step 3: Design an area of safety for You

You probably already desire solitude at some point Why not tap into the desire to create a space of safety and security for you? You can accomplish this by making a sanctuary for your ground in your home, or creating a space outside of your home you love to go to. If you'd like to go all out it is possible to do both!

If you are looking to create a tranquil space at home, you should consider selecting a room or an space in the same room that you can decorate the space with items that relax and provide a sense of grounding. Make use of stones, plants soothing incenses, soft textiles with uplifting images, and other relaxing and soothing instruments to create a more welcoming space. Begin to practice your daily routine of grounding within that particular area of your home on a regular basis. What will happen is that you will find yourself more in touch with the area in question, and even the act of entering it will be a moment of grounding, making the intention of grounding in the sanctuary more potent.

If you're looking to include a place in your routine of grounding, think about selecting one close to home and one that you are able to visit regularly. A nearby park or bird sanctuary could provide a wonderful chance to locate an area where you can relax and get grounded in. This type of location for grounding is especially beneficial when you is finding that their home can be a place of stress or unsettling energies.

Step 4: Make Experiences Richer

One way you can integrate your gifts in your everyday life is by making your experience more enjoyable by utilizing your other senses. Consider the following scenario: if you could experience another person's feelings and energies that are deeply, think about what you could experience as in a profound way? Consider how deeply you enjoy meals, laughter nostalgia, and peace. Find ways to lift yourself by these events and try to discover ones that consistently make you feel happier, especially in the event of difficulties in your day. When you do this you not only create a great opportunity to live the joy of life as well, it lets you begin to find opportunities that will consistently bring you from a tense mood.

Your Quick Start Step: Feel intensely

Your first step now is to locate an event that you can completely take part in and let yourself be carried by it, just as you are by the energy of others or feelings when you're not secure and grounded. Choose an activity that you can completely immerse yourself in, and then see what energy and energy levels you take away from it and what it is like. If you begin to feel overwhelming or overwhelming Take a moment to settle yourself before returning to the activity or switching to something that is more calm.

The more you are able to practice getting the most enjoyment from life by utilizing your energy in this way more positive your life will be overall. It's worth the time to begin learning to be mindful and fully engaged with every moment of your life, so that you break the habit of escaping and dissociating yourself from your experience. This will allow you to reconnect with your everyday life and begin living in your own way and not just for the people around you.

Chapter 7: The Structure Of The Enneagram Diagram

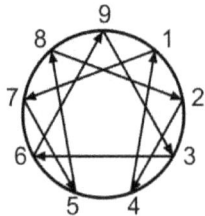

The first step to comprehending the world and those that surrounds you is to know your own self. This is a task which many people have difficulty with. There's a lot we don't know about us and, as a result of that opacity in our efforts to understand others around us becomes nearly impossible. It's impossible to search for something you don't understand, for what can you tell if you've found it when you don't even know what you were supposed to be searching for at all?

Knowing the enneagram system will lead you on an exciting adventure, a trip into self-discovery. The amazing human qualities will be enlightening, amaze you and , in some cases likely make you shiver. You'll discover that there's plenty you did not know about you. It will help you see new possibilities and inspire you to acknowledge your limitations the challenges, strengths, and the influences within your surroundings that inspire or inspire you.

When you explore the enneagram, you'll discover a variety of things you can apply to your day-to-day life. As we said earlier that when you discover more about yourself, you can open your mind to new possibilities and also learn to appreciate people better as you view them from an enlightened and new perspective.

Understanding the enneagram's structure can bring positive changes to your life and provide you a fresh lease on life. The enneagram's structure may seem complicated however, it's an extremely simple concept. It's a meshwork made of a triangle as well as an irregular hexagram in the shape of a circle. The most effective way to appreciate the simpleness of this design is by drawing it your self.

With a compass, draw an outline of a circle. Mark 9 points along the circumference of the circle. Each is one an equal distance from the other. The circle is

360 degrees, so take 40 degrees, and mark a point. Then repeat until you have nine points marks along the circumference of the circle.

Each point should be labeled with a number (1 9 - 1)) with nine being on highest. This is the first step to identify the personality types of nine.

Before we think about the triangle or the hexagon, this basic design should already provide a basic understanding of the structure of human personality. Every aspect of life is a circle. If you do not delve deep into the theory behind the enneagram, it is likely that you will be able comprehend how interdependence works as well as the entire.

When you've completed the enneagram, you'll notice that the points are connected by smaller lines in the diagram. If you look closer, and you'll see an equilateral triangle inside the circle. It is a triangle that has the angles of all 3 sides equally that is made up of the points 3, 6 and 9. The other six points join to create an irregular hexagonal.

What we can see in this diagram are nine personality types that are all connected in the same way. What do these numbers tell you about you? It's a sign that, in your total have all nine personalities that may manifest in a way. When you look back on your life, and your choices and you realize that you are a amount of each one of them. But there will be one type of personality that is over the rest. The dominant type is the one that determines your personality. It is the basis of your personality.

Personalities are innate. They develop from childhood and as you grow older, you take on your character and go forward to be who you have become today. Every person is born with a blank slate. Through the years, a variety of writers and specialists on the enneagram have tried to unravel the mystery of personality types. Although each expert has their own perspective, they all consider that every person is born with a particular personality kind.

Your inborn personality is what gives you your identity. It is through this that you discover how to be a part of your surroundings and interact with those you meet, what you do not like, and what things you enjoy. The choices that we make are the result from our unconscious mind. It is also true that the subconscious mind is affected by your personality. This is the reason you may form certain relationships with your family members and your parents, yet you have a different view of authority and react differently to affection than others.

The development process and personality are closely linked. At the point when children reach six years old and begin to exhibit distinctive behavior and responses to various changes that occur in their life. Their identity becomes clear and they begin to embrace an opportunity to decide their roles within the society.

Typically, the type of personality that you are able to identify with is the result of many different changes that occur during your the time you were a child. Apart from genetics, this also includes the environment you grow into, pivotal moments of your life and any other factors that could have influenced your growth or development in the way. This is why it's safe to say that there is no way to change their personality one type to the next. There are small fragments of all personality types that we have within us. They are reflected in different ways in the ways we react to various situations. This means it's probable that one or more of your less appealing personality types could suddenly emerge or perhaps you're in uncharted territory, and it is the only way to adjust. But, the dominant personality type will continue to be dominant and continue to be dominant.

The concept that a person is dominant in is often a false notion. If you take the term 'dominant' as a definition one would think that this type of personality will rule your life every day. But, that's not the reality. When you take a look at the traits and descriptions that make up your predominant personality, you'll find it impossible to exhibit each one constantly. Some traits could be subtle, while others are obvious, which means you may not be able to experience the entirety of your personality in all instances.

The majority of personality traits can be expressed as a reaction to something or someone that we call an emotional reaction. Your response to conflicts at home may differ from your response to conflicts at work. The same principle applies to how you display affection and the way you treat individuals. Your stage or position in life also determines the way you express yourself.

Cultural affiliations can also can affect your personalitydue to moral convictions and differences in the beliefs of different the different cultures. It is important to understand that no one is superior to other people. The numerical meaning is an impartial designation that eliminates any bias. The number 9 doesn't suggest that the individual is superior to a number 3.

There are certain traits that every culture holds with esteem. If you display these characteristics in your character and character, you will be appreciated in these communities. The normal reaction in the situation is to accept the love and awe and, with time will become an automatic reaction to you. But, you can't be too generous with any thing without consequences, isn't it? Look at someone who truly cares about alleviating the suffering of other people. Although you could do your best to assist others but you cannot be doing it constantly. It's going to take a toll on you over time even if you appear to perform an act of charity, you'll face an uphill battle in the other areas of your life as a consequence of your kindnesses.

The same is true of personality kinds. The more you know about them, the more clear your understanding will be. But, understanding of personality types isn't sufficient until you're aware of their weaknesses. The traits and personalities of people are recognized by different cultures in various ways. Does this mean that certain people are more desirable than others? It's not true. What we can take away about this situation is every society has its own unique reward scheme that values certain particular traits of some individuals more than other people.

What does this mean for you? What can you do to improve your life? The answer is simple: self-awareness. Be aware of what you're about and what you are living for. Discover and master the various personality kinds. Discover which type of personality you are and the traits you can identify with.

Why is this so important? It is a society in which people struggle to make a mark. Because of social media, everyone is focused on appearances, looks and opinions. A lot of people live in the shadows of their peers and not because they're obliged to or forced to, but simply because that it is one of the best ways to achieve satisfaction and happiness. But this is an error. Any imitation that is a copycat under another name simply an imitation. If you attempt to present yourself as something or else, you will only succeed in creating a perfect illusion. Every time you fail to grasp your real self. If you mimic someone for too long, you could lose track of your identity, or feel embarrassed of the person you really are.

Self-awareness means realizing your own self. You will discover the things that make you tick and why you do what you do and as a result learning to recognize your role in the world. You will appreciate your worth and what others are worth in your life.

Finding Your Personality Type

We know that there are only nine distinct personality types, determining the type that best describes you isn't so easy. The human character of a person is not always white and black. In addition to the nine major personality types, here are just some of the additional aspects that play into the equation:

* Subtypes

In any of the personality categories there are three variations. So, theoretically there are 27 distinct features that you'll be able to determine your own. But, since some of them have close resemblances, this is not the most straightforward tasks to accomplish.

* Wings

The term "Wings" in this context refers to the related types that are on either side of a personality type. If you study further about the different personality types, you'll discover that every personality is associated with at some point with similar people. This can have a significant impact on your life, even though it's not as strong as the dominant personality. In some instances the two personality types could have an impact on your life.

* Arrows/lines

Arrows are a reference to the direction you'd like your typical behavior to follow in relation to the environment around you, regardless of whether you're at ease or are in a stressful situation.

* Development level

Your personality type develops is also dependent on the level of your personal development and growth. The people who are more developed generally have various stages of maturity, and in this case, it is difficult to determine what category they belong to. These individuals may exhibit diverse traits in each persona due to the fact that they draw information from their experiences and shared experiences. This means they can manage their lives and blend into or adjust to various situations effortlessly.

With all the issues mentioned above what can you do to make sure that you're taking a fair chance of understanding and accepting your individuality? The following article will equip you with the necessary information to do this.

Be open to new ideas

At the beginning, you'll have to eliminate your personal prejudices towards tests, or anything else associated with this procedure. You must accept the tests and complete the tests in the correct way. Be sure to be prompt when answering the questions. When you've gotten the results and have an understanding of your predominant persona is, make sure you don't rest on your laurels.

There could be some aspect of your personality isn't in line with the beliefs you had previously held. It could alter your view of your personality particularly if you're having doubts about your personality.

Do not obsess about kinds!

If you are reading about various personalities and their distinct traits, it is easy to think about certain types with the assumption that they're superior to other types. The problem is that you'll forget the crucial facts. These personality tests aren't about the various types of personality; they're about you.

Do not look at this issue from the perspective of the traits you would like to see you could have. It is not about assigning yourself a specific type; you're trying to figure what you are according to your current preferences.

Personal bias

It is typical for people to be sunk with preconceived notions about themselves while researching the enneagram personality kinds. Most often, they avoid revealing certain characteristics they perceive as negative. If you don't admit to these traits they won't give an accurate perception of who you are. Be aware that personality tests will only provide the most accurate or close to accurate outcome if you supply them with exact information.

The risk of confusion

When you are learning about personalities, you should be ready for some unclear outcomes. Particularly the peacemaker and loyalists are two categories which are easy to confuse because their characteristics are fairly universal. They may be representative of nearly all other personality types and, therefore, you may struggle to point them out.

In addition both categories don't have distinct characteristics which you can easily identify with. If you're already conflicted over a couple of categories, the vagueness of the loyaltyist and peacemaker could further confuse you.

Chapter 8: Physical Appearance

Did you realize that your appearance can give other people a clue of your personality? Anyone who is one particular type of Enneagram are likely to have a few physical characteristics in addition. This section you'll discover the physical characteristics of each of the types.

Type One

The physical appearance among the Ones is a sign that is a sign of their inner dryness. The majority of them are slim and lean sometimes even to the extremes. Males are more likely to have the look of a mustache or beard. In extreme instances, Ones can be obese however, it's extremely uncommon. They tend to be tall, straight and make only a few gestures. People with this type of personality appear unassuming and rigid. Their smiles are usually controlled, however when they smile, it's always authentic. People like order and cleanliness which is evident in their appearance, too.

Type Two

Twos usually choose outfits that are simple but fashionable. A sense of style is crucial for twos. Twos are usually elegant, well-dressed and are known to add some shade to their attire by wearing something subtle and distinctive, such as a vibrant tie or an accessory of statement jewelry. In a social setting, Twos seem a little formal. Both women and men who have this

Enneagram type are dressed in a professional manner at all times.

Type Three

Threes love to dress the best they can. Their outfits are appropriate and reflect current trends in fashion. Threes are aware of their weight and will not let them become overweight. Their clothes usually reflect their calm and joyful temperament. Threes are also known to be pretty and sexy.

Type Four

Fours prefer to show themselves to the world in a way that is artistic and elegantly. Their style of dressing typically is the combination of black and other uplifting shades. They generally have a moderate build. Did you see people and women in extravagant costumes? If you have it's highly likely they're Four or Seven (more on this later).

Type Five

Fives usually aren't very enthused about their appearance. The most appropriate description of a Five is to describe them as normal, reasonable and not overly exaggerated. A majority of the Fives appear to wear glasses. Fives are known to sport the look of a sloppy one. Fives with an energizing Four wing are known to be attracted by attractive clothing items. There's a high possibility that a person who has messy hair and oddly shaped glasses is a Type Five.

Type Six

Sixes are naturally inclined to be liked and attractive. There are only two extremes Sixes can be - they could either be extremely attractive or shabby and have nothing else. Sixes are known to show as tough, even though they're not. It's not intentional and their manner of speaking can come to appear hostile or accusatory.

Type Seven

Sevens can be very giddy however their clothes are generally gender-neutral. Sevens are a color-loving bunch and are always looking to stand out. They aren't as able to display the sophistication that Fours have in terms of fashion. Therefore, the clothes Sevens choose to wear are usually extravagant and loud. It's not something that Sevens should be concerned about.

Type Eight

Eights require a lot of attention to their appearance. Clean and stylish are two adjectives that best describe an eight. The way they dress is contingent on their mood and the circumstances. For instance, if an Eight is content and confident and confident, he appears stylish and elegant. If he's not happy or isn't feeling happy, it's exactly the opposite. The mood of eight determines how they show themselves. The majority of them have big features and a rough and rough appearance.

Type Nine

Nines are typically physically massive. They have large and strong bones. Their movements are smooth and graceful when they're at their best. If they are Nine is in a state of disarray the most often, they come across as being uncoordinated and clumsy. Their clothes are typically classic and they are rarely extravagant or flashy. Nines don't need attention and their fashion reflects the same.

However, it's not simple to recognize an Enneagram-related type just by the appearance of their face. However, the tips that are discussed in this chapter can be useful in identifying people and the Enneagram. When you've learned to recognize Enneagram types, you'll soon be able find some physical similarities between the different varieties.

Chapter 9: Type I The Reformer

The Type One Reformers have a constant mission to make a difference in the world. They work to overcome obstacles. Additionally, they're known as perfectionists. Some are activists seeking an acceptable reason for their mission of what they think they need to do to improve the world.

People with Type One personality are extremely meticulous and ethical. They have a clear sense of what is morally acceptable, and what is not or unacceptable. A lot of Type One people become teachers as well as activists, advocates, and advocates for positive change. Their aim is to improve the world and the people around them, and to avoid making mistakes. They are organized, disciplined and may be extremely demanding of people in their lives. They strive to keep high standards, which may cause them to criticize others and look like an idealist. They are usually plagued by anger and resentment. They are sensitive and noble, realist and shrewd at their most effective. They respect morality and adhere to them better than most people.

For an idealist, the chance of making mistakes is a major worry and fear for those who are Type One personalities. The primary goal of Type One personalities is to be in balance, possess integrity, and a general conviction that they are doing what is right and ethical.

The most well-known One individuals are those who have left their comfortable lives for the greater wellbeing of other people. They seek out incredible adventures and achieve extraordinary results to benefit other people. And even Type Ones on a lesser degree still want to help others as well as to the natural world.

On a negative note, Type Ones are constantly justifying their behavior to themselves as well as to other people.

They constantly beat themselves for their mistakes or mistakes.

If you're an individual who constantly listens to the persistent and unforgiving voice that is in your mind Learn to distinguish your self-worth from the voice. Instead, you should learn from your mistakes you make, accept that you will not be always perfect and you'll be able to utilize your inner voice for development.

A Type One person with a Nine-wing personality is more idealist. They might use their thoughts to justify their actions. Fear of being judged by anyone keeps them from criticism. An Type One with a Two-wing transforms into an advocate. They know the best way to aid others and enhance their surroundings.

Stress Point

The Typ Ones feel stressed. They might exhibit unhealthy features associated with Type Four personalities.

Some of these harmful behaviors could be:

Depression

Avoidance

Narcissism

Despair

Feelings of hopelessness

Shame

Security Point

In the event that Type Ones experience periods of growth, they can exhibit typical to healthy-level characteristics of Type Seven personalities.

Some of these traits that are healthy could include:

Grateful

Appreciative

Joyful

Prove the value of living

Enthusiastic

Extroverted

Practical

Productive

Stages 1 of Type 1.

Levels 1 and 2 are considered good levels for development. Be aware that the characteristics displayed in these levels could be observed by Type Fours at different stages of development.

Niveaus 3-4, and 5 are considered to be average levels of development.

Levels 6, 7 , and 8 are considered to be unhealthy developmental levels. Be aware that the characteristics displayed in these levels may be observed by those who have Type Sevens in periods of stress.

Health:

Level 1

Extraordinary insight and discernment

They are able to recognize the reality of their situation and can determine the best method of action in every circumstance.

Level 2

Convictions that are reliable and personal

Their view about right and wrong is in line with their moral and religious values. They strive to be rational and rational, as well as self-controlled, to find the balance and maturity of all aspects.

Level 3

High-quality principles

They aim to be honest, fair and impartial. Truth and justice are their main values.

Their passion as well as their responsibility and integrity aid in teaching others, and also to speak out for the truth.

Average:

Level 4

Idealist critics, crusaders and supporters.

They're not happy with the reality. They make it their personal mission to make everything better. They are the ones who are continuously serving multiple causes. They have a clear sense of what they believe that things should be.

Level 5

Fearful of making mistakes

Everything has to be in line with their goals. They are organized, but distant and distant emotionally. They do not let their feelings or impulses dictate their behavior or their actions in any manner. They are hardworking who are punctual and demanding.

Level 6

Judgmental perfectionists

They tend to be extremely opinionated about everything , causing them to become extremely critical of themselves and the people they surround themselves with. They are constantly harsh to those who are unable to meet their ideals of excellence. They may appear aggressive and uncaring.

Unhealthy

Level 7

Dogmatic

They are rigid as well as intolerant and self-righteous. They believe that they are the only ones who is right. They're strict with their judgment but they justify the actions of others.

Level 8

Hypocritical

They dwell on the flaws as well as the mistakes that others have made however, they fail to notice their own mistakes.

Level 9

Obsessive-compulsive disorders and depressive personality disorders are frequent mental health problems. Patients may suffer from massive depression or even a breakdown in their nervous system. They may push other people away in order to isolate themselves from their own shortcomings.

Chapter 10: Instinctual Variants

Now that we've outlined the traits that all nine types within the Enneagram are, you might believe you have a clear understanding of the type you're in and what to do from this point. Perhaps you're more confused. You might have recognized several types or recognized yourself in some of them.

That's why we'll discuss certain aspects that could alter your base Enneatype. Knowing Wings as well as Instinctual Variants can help you better understand your personality kind.

Wings

The most well-known Enneagram researchers and experts adhere to and propagate the notion that the personality of an individual is affected and altered by either or both Enneatypes in close proximity to their personal. This is why they refer to "Wings," as in the type of personality that sits that is a wing of the main personality type. For instance, if you're Seven, your wing could be six, eight or even a combination of both.

It is possible that you specifically and exclusively identify with one particular type. This is fine. It's rare for someone to be solely depicted by one Enneatype however most people are a principal type. The Wing could be described as the second element of your personality or the other aspect of it. If you really would like to reach a an understanding of your own personality and the way you interact with other people, you'll need to be aware of Wing and the Wing of the dominant type influences your personality.

The majority of people are believed to be most affected by one of their wings however, technically, due to the structure of this system everyone has elements of both wings. Most of the time the truth is that each person will have their very own predominant type and then an especially significant wings. There is also the possibility to be defined equally by two distinct Enneatypes. This is called having balanced wings and although it's not exactly popular, it's not uncommon.

Many claim to experience the appearance and awakening second wings' as they get older. It is thought this is a part of the natural aging process and development process. It is also believed that as one ages and develops, they accumulate increasing amounts of experiences, acquire greater wisdom, and attain an understanding that is more balanced. In this regard it is quite possible that instead of changing into a different type of Enneatype, or creating a different wings, the older people could simply have the experience and insight to recognize other Enneatypes not necessarily their personal.

However, Wings aren't one of the primary Ennea modifier. We'll then discover our natural instincts as well as how they're classified and what they say about us.

Instinctual Subtypes

Enneatypes allow us to define the main traits that govern our behavior in everyday life, but everyone is at times reacting or acting according to our gut instinct. What does this mean for the personality of us? Does our instinct play a greater influence on the character that we are?

The short answer is that yes our instincts play a significant role in determining our personality. But it's not as complex as it appears. We can basically categorize the instinct into three subtypes, which we call Instinctual Subtypes. The nine types of Enneatype may be modified by one of the three types of Instinctual Subtypes which gives an overall total of 27 different personality subtypes that are represented through the Enneagram.

The first type is the Self-Preservation Subtype. those who are born with this tend to achieve independence and peace of mind. The people who have this type are likely to give the highest focus in their lives on things that contribute to their wellbeing. They're likely to be concerned with their health, perhaps their home, or maybe their financial situation. It's not unusual to find people who have this subtype to be extremely focused on the various aspects mentioned above. They generally seek out social interaction less than other people. That's not to say that they do not enjoy it, but they don't have the same needs that others do. Most often, people who are self-protection tend to be more closed emotionally than other people and could appear less sociable or relaxed.

Another instinctual Subtype can be described as one of Social Subtype. These are the people who have a great time when they work in a group or in a group. They function well as groups and are generally helpful as well as cooperative and collaborative. This is a positive aspect to bring to an organization, since when an issue arises Social Variants will quickly get the group together to resolve the issue by working together. However, they should be cautious about their motivations, as their inherent desire to be part of groups often leads to an urge to be a leader in a group. This naturally is positive and healthy as every team requires an effective leader However, they must remain cautious to not be too domineering or overbearing.

Then, there's The Sexual Variant, sometimes called the One-to-One Variant. It is important to remember that the instincts of a Sexual Variant aren't always about sexual intimacy, however it plays a significant and frequent part. A sexual variant is one who seeks one-on-one intimacy, and is often sated sexually. You can imagine, Sexual Subtypes are the most intense out of all three Subtypes They are also known to be a lot of fun however they can be a slightly on the emotional volatile side. Engaging in relationships is usually the top priority for sexual Variants, but they need to be cautious to only be in positive relationships. In general, sexual subtypes tend to be a bit more prone to get into conflict, and can have a tendency to be less enthused by the traditional rules and obligations.

Chapter 11: The Center Of Yourself

Centers represent the various types of relationships. Centers represent the various kinds and connections

the similarities and differences between the two. In the end,

these concerns orbit a dominant, quite unconscious,

an expression of disconnection with the central

The self. The inner self is a source of rage and the emotional hub is a source of shame.

The Intellectual Center gives us fear. The nine types of personality contain these emotional states.

However, in every Center the actions of the different types are determined by the Center's

Theme.

The level of emotion that each person experiences determines the coping mechanism our individual uses.

What exactly does that mean? Now we will discover the kinds of emotions that

They guide them, and how it determines how we are shaped.

A. The Inherent Rage Rage

Eights, Nines and one are all based on the "gut sensation" process, which is well-defined. They are guided

through the body, usually by the body, often. the Boss (8) can help

It is important to recognize that you are not alone! They could speak loudly or move but they don't feel

You must get permission to their actions. We have a mediator (9) is going to do all he can to

They are unable to express their indifference to their. People who are the Perfectionist (1) remain in denial about their anger. known for their denial of their anger.

Repressing their anger. Instead, they concentrate on their relationships and the world around them,

putting their negative energy to build their egos.

They are a in our daily life. You will surely be able to imagine

Someone in school who always stood in the right direction. It's not difficult to

Remember someone who always provided an open and safe space for people to be able to communicate.

Focus on the negative aspects of life, or concentrate on the positives and take action on it.

the emotions. It is trained to creating positive energy.

B. The Emotional Shame

The Twos Threes Fours, Twos and Threes Fours are in search of positive energy, which is why they feel loved and appreciated. It's the case that

Simple concept that helps them control their shameful feelings. For example,

(2) The assistant (2) can do all they can to convince anyone that they are great

People. The more they are loved, the less their feelings of shame be.

Three (3) Doers Doer (3) is an easy to understand. Their actions speak more louder than anythingelse, and

They'll show that they are trustworthy and compassionate people. They will appear to others as if they are trustworthy and caring.

Eccentric (4) look at their extraordinary talents and capabilities.

Overshadow any shame they might be feeling.

Our emotional individuals to keep our eyes focused on the greatest things life can offer.

If a bleak situation occurs it is possible to trust The Emotionals to create a positive outcome.

alternative, positive solution is accessible which they are proud of.

C."The Intellectual The Intellectual Fear

Fives, Sixes and Sevens will provide you with the complete picture of an issue. The

Watchers (5) appreciate their privacy and want to be independent. Their motivation is

focused on understanding the world with the intention of becoming involved with confidence. They also tend to be engaged in their private lives

Complex worlds. A Loved Skeptic (6) is similar to the beehive. They're full of fear.

You just want security, and are working to find it in a variety of ways, including financial,

Professional and spiritual. Professional and spiritual. Epicure (7) creates excitement to fear, by ensuring

engaged in a variety of stimulating projects. They'll be able to avoid injury or defeat and will be

Deprivation, even if it is a way of avoiding.

Our wonderful Intellectuals are our most experienced analysts. You can trust them to examine from every angle, and then give the most confident answer due to their fear of not being adequate. You

Are safe in their competent in the hands of their skilled.

D. Fly High

You can score extremely across different types within the same Center due to the fact that they

We share traits of personality and behavior. To be able to understand one another be able to

Be aware you are aware that The Wing bears an influence. The Wing is a reference to the persona on both sides of the dominant in each of the two sides of our dominant. For example, suppose you're a Perfectionist

(1) (1). You will be in a strong connection with (1), you will be able to strongly relate with Assistant (2) in addition to and The Mediator (9).

Certain people who are older might develop what is known as the Second Wing. This

This is particularly true especially for those looking for the practice of spiritual healing or therapy. This is especially true for those seeking spiritual or therapeutic work.

thanks to our elders learning more about the world, our world , and their role within the equation. It's possible to say that knowing your personality is just the first step.

There's more to knowing about The Enneagram than just a number or

Illustrations with an outline of a circle, and pointed lines in all directions. Our

The human body develops in stages. This is the case for our psyche.

Chapter 12: The Enneagram Type Personality 1 The Reformer

This type of personality is also known as "the Perfectionist as well as the Refiner. Type 1s are motivated by the need to do the right thing or be the best. The desire to be better or others, or even circumstances are always focused on repairing mistakes. This persona is obsessed with the possibility of improvement. They always look for ways to improve their lives because for Type 1s there is never a thing that is good enough, which is why they are sometimes referred to as perfectionists. Due to their responsibilities Reformers are often able to take on more responsibilities in service and jobs such as health workers, teachers and ministers.

What makes a The Reformer a Super Personality?

The Reformer is a person with an extremely high moral standards. They are very responsible and competent acquaintances, colleagues and partners. They are also highly loyal individuals who are highly principled and knowledgeable. Their strength is due to the fact that they are able to adhere to rules and demand others in their circle to follow them too.

Since they're so firm in their beliefs They are usually exceptional leaders with the capacity to motivate others to live up to their ideals of excellence.

The Reformer is extremely self-controlled. They are natural lists makers and organizers. They are also highly focused and ambitious, usually being classified as workers. They are pragmatic and proactive people who complete tasks. They are usually the last person to leave their office and the first to get up each day.

They have a keen sense of detail. The person who is the Reformer excels at organizing chaos because of their capacity to spot flaws in other people their own lives, as well as situations. This is beneficial in improving and seeking solutions.

The Reformer is accountable. Since the Reformer is an intelligent, calm person, they're excellent potential moderators between groups who don't have an elevated level of consciousness. Due to their responsibility Reformers also tend to put off their pleasures, waiting until all their obligations and tasks have been accomplished and checked before they can participate in any activity solely in order to have fun.

Die Deadly Sins of Reformers

Reformers are stifling in their control of themselves. Due to the Reformers' desire to be perfect They often feel guilt for not meeting their expectations they have for themselves as well as the expectations others place on them of them could be unattainable. This can lead to anger at themselves as well as the world that surrounds them. Reformers often suppress this anger since it is perceived as an unwholesome emotion, and they are genuinely trying to be perfect. In the absence of suppression it is not uncommon for Reformers to have a burst of temper outbursts. In the majority of cases the anger manifests into other emotions , like anger, frustration, and annoyance and a judgmental mindset. Refraining from anger can be detrimental to the relationships the reformer builds as their interactions with other people may come across as harsh and negative.

Reformers suffer from emotional repression. Because of their constant striving for perfection, they are unable to enjoy taking a break and frequently deny themselves the pleasures of everyday life. It is a strain on their emotional health which is why Reformers tend to suppress their emotions as they are unable to being able to express them. The reason for this is their belief that showing emotions is a sign of insecurity and inability to control. Type 1s aren't often spontaneous, even though they possess the ability to have many interests and talents , and rarely ever have nothing to accomplish.

Reformers are demanding absolute perfection. They always seek perfection in both themselves and in others. Because of this, and the ability to suppress their emotions, they make reformers difficult to deal with due to their strict standards and their cold attitude towards others when their desire of perfection has not been fulfilled.

Reformers suffer from judgemental tendencies. Because they have such an eye for detail and want everything to be "perfect," they over examine themselves and others and this can be quite stressful for the Reformer as well as the people who are around them.

How do Reformers relate to other Personality Types

Reformers Versus. Type 2s

Reformers are very compatible with Type 2s, which is also known as Helpers. Actually, they're an ideal pair. If a bond in any way is created between two of these personalities, it is founded on the basis of shared values. Helpers bring nurturing and compassionate characteristics to relationships while Type 1s are responsible for consistency, integrity, and consistency. Despite the wonderful complementarity however, there is a possibility of conflict between the two personalities due to the fact that Reformers are prone to be at work first, play later, and maintain their own and other people extremely in control. However Helpers may view this as too solitary.

Reformers Versus. Type 3s

These two personalities are knowledgeable, focused and goal-oriented. Together they can achieve many amazing things due to their energy and desire to achieve. There is trouble when there is a connection between one of the types and the other the type 3 who is the more successful, since they lack emotional connection to one another and are prone to becoming rivals. There is also the possibility of conflict because reformers are extremely ethical and type 3s don't want to cut corners to get the job completed faster and easier.

Reformers Vs. Type 4s

Due to their tendency towards depression, the type ones often are mistaken as Type 4s, who are Artists However, type 1s are not as indulgent as Type 4s. They are alike in that they both have a sense of idealism and dedicated to doing what is right and good within the universe. However, bringing them together is similar to mixing oil and water because , while type 1 is rational and objective, type 2 tends to look at things from a personal perspective.

Reformers Versus. Type 5s

Due to their intelligence and independent, they are frequently confused with type 5s, who are deeply thought-provoking and tend to stay in their own space and observe instead of engaging. Reformers are active but they are not ones who relax and think. Both are typically emotionally detached and have a difficult time to alter their basic beliefs about life. So, creating a bond between these two personalities is often a challenge.

Reformers Vs. Type 6s

Type 1s also get confused with to be type 6s. Type 6s tend to be hard-working, anxious and serious-minded individuals, but they differ in the type of emotional bonds they establish with their peers as well as the direction that comes from their internal feeling of purpose. Type 1s are very rational and have a clear mind. They are extremely confident in their decisions and adept at thinking clearly even when under stress. So, they tend to lead. Type 6s are, however prefer to follower since they are stressed out and are extremely unsure of their ability to make decisions. The relationship between these two types of personality isn't easy to build due to the fact that type 1s exert too much pressure on those who are type 6s. This could lead to resentment, and a lot of disagreements.

Reformers Versus. Type 7s

The Type 7 personality type is known as the Enthusiast , and is remarkably distinct from Reformer. Actually, both personalities can be viewed as being opposites. However, it's the opposing traits that can create a connection between them. complementary as they each bring something valuable for the team. Type 1s provide orderliness, a sense of prudence and a keen eye for detail and a high level of quality while Enthusiasts have enthusiasm, energy, and the desire to explore different things and to not be obsessed with the pursuit of perfection. Naturally, because of the same reason, a relation between these two types of personality might be difficult to establish.

Reformers Vs. Type 8s

Two personality types share an underlying commonality in both fight to defend what's right and fair. They are both Protectors of the weak , and are determined to change things. A connection between them is very effective as it is built with a clear understanding of mission, and is direct and decisive. Although a connection between them is likely, it's not often that they make a romantic couple. They are able to function as colleagues or as friends since they both desire to have the upper hand even though they differ on the method used in order to complete a task. They're both self-contained and controlled and are unable to express their feelings.

Reformers Vs. Type 9s

Both of these personalities are eager to bring about an improvement in the society. They both ignore their personal desires and strive to improve the lives of other people. They each believe in the concept of delayed satisfying. The difference lies in how they approach conflict and conflicts. When type 1s are in a state of frustration by their situation and display a judgemental attitude Type 9s tend to retreat and shut down and avoid having to talk about their emotions. When there is a connection between these two types of personalities this could create an atmosphere of anger and the building up to an blast of anger.

How the Reformer can Enhance his or her life

The Reformer can make improvements in their life by accepting themselves. One must recognize that despite having several strengths, they have weaknesses, and that's completely normal. Alongside acknowledging that they are not perfect, they need to be more self-respecting. By becoming more mindful, the Reformer to be more comfortable with their own shortcomings and more understanding of their desires. There are a variety of actions Reformers can use to get more aware of their emotions.

Most of these practices require opening chakras, or chakra meditation. There are many different kinds of chakra meditation and all have the capacity to channel energy to specific locations within your body. The effects they produce is enhanced by the sounds that are made using Sanskrit letters. Chanting causes resonance within the body, so that you feel the chakra's movement. The two most commonly used letters that you can sing include "A," which is pronounced as "ah," and "M" which is pronounced "mng" ("ng" as"ng" as in "king").

Without further delay Here are some ways the Reformer can accomplish these:

* Practice meditation on the sacral chakra. This helps the Reformer to be more

connected to their feelings and experience feelings of enthusiasm. The method of performing the sacral chakra meditation is easy. Relax in a calm space and relax. Place both hands onto your laps with your palms facing upwards. The left hand goes under that of the hand on your left. The thumb's tip should touch gently. Focus on the sensation of your back. Then take a slow breath out and in and chanting each exhale for a maximum of 10 breaths. This will allow you to activate your sacral chakra, which is located at the sacral bone that is located at the base of your spine.

* Do the heart chakra. This kind of meditation can help the Reformer grow in compassion for him self and other people as well. For this kind of meditation on

chakras, place your feet on the floor and sit on them cross-legged. Place your index fingers and your thumb to meet in both hands. Put one hand to your knee, and the right hand below your breastbone, which is a little over your solar plexus. You can chant while focusing on the chakra of your heart at your spine that is aligned with your heart.

* Make use of Acupressure. Acupressure is a different method of treatment that involves the application of pressure to specific points on the body which are believed to be energy lines. It is a method that has been used for a long time and can help promote relaxation and overall well-being. The practitioners of Acupressure who are licensed professionals, utilize

their palms, fingers, elbows or feet for applying the pressure, while the client is completely clothed on a soft table. Reformers may find relief through this technique if they stimulates the LIV-3 muscle, which is located inside the foot along the line connecting the large toe with second. This stimulates relaxation and releases feelings like anger or repressed. The SP-6 point which is situated in the inner part in the leg's lower part, just below the ankle may get stimulated and re-energised to reduce stress, relax and lessen the irritability.

* Do mindful yoga. Mindful yoga is a method of application of the traditional Buddhist mindfulness techniques to link the breath and mind. It allows the

participant to fully experience the present moment. The yoga practice we'll be discussing in this article is known as the Hero's posture. To start take a kneeling position and then sit on your heels. Then, with your hands resting on your thighs and lengthen the tailbone towards the ceiling. Expand your collar bones to the point that the shoulder blades slide toward each other with ease. This opens your chest. Keep this posture for one minute. Let your mind clear and be focused on the peaceful breaths.

Other strategies that the Reformer may employ to enhance his or her life can include:

* Devoting time in the day to be with themselves when there is no reason to

accomplish any other thing than to stay connected to their thoughts and thoughts.

• Keep a diary so that they can record the thoughts and feelings of theirs, which aids introspection and reflection.

* Participating in group therapy to help develop their feelings and realize that no one else will judge their issues and needs like everybody else.

* Learning patience when they share their wisdom and knowledge to other people.

* Developing a sense of their anger at their own failings and the weaknesses of others in order to reduce their self-criticism and undermine the effectiveness of the work of others.

* Be mindful of the words they use in their conversations with other people so that they don't seem to be judging.

* Learn to channel their angry feelings in a positive manner since repressing anger is not just a cause of an unhealthy mental and emotional environment , but also a negative physical health, such as hypertension and ulcers.

* Sometimes, indulge on a little treat to enjoy it.

Conclusion

After you've come to comprehend the nine Enneagram people along with the many possibilities they could be harnessed You may have gotten an accurate picture of who you truly are. It is likely that you can connect with a variety of different types of personalities however, one type is more authentic to you than the other.

Many feel that understanding the specifics of the Enneagram can open their eyes and gives the reason for their actions or for the actions of those around them. When you are able to understand the underlying principles of the Enneagram it will allow you to look at everything around you through new eyes. You'll embark on a path of self-discoveryand discover things about your own self that you never believed existed, but were under the surface.

www.ingramcontent.com/pod-product-compliance
Lightning Source LLC
Chambersburg PA
CBHW071837080526
44589CB00012B/1026